Roller Skating

by Eileen Kulper

**Published By
Capstone Press, Inc.
Mankato, Minnesota USA**

Distributed By

CP CHILDRENS PRESS®
CHICAGO

CIP
LIBRARY OF CONGRESS CATALOGING IN PUBLICATION DATA

Kulper, Eileen.
    Roller skating / by Eileen Kulper.
        p. cm. – (Action sports)
    Summary: Explores the world of roller skating, including such aspects as competitive skating, artistic skating, and speed skating.

    ISBN 1-56065-050-8:
    1. Roller-skating – Juvenile literature. (1. Roller skating.) I. Title. II. Series.
    GV859.K85   1989
    796.2'1 – dc20   89-29550
                                                          CIP
                                                          AC

PHOTO CREDITS

National Museum of Rollerskating: 15, 30, 32
Steven Manufacturing Co.: 9, 48
Steve Priest: 4, 7, 26, 35

CAPSTONE PRESS
Box 669, Mankato, MN 56001

Contents

Saturday Night Roller Skating

It is 8:00 pm on a Saturday night. In the dressing room a skater makes some last minute adjustments. She watches competitors around her do the same. She checks the wheel action on her skates and adjusts them slightly. Re-tying her laces again, she waits. In front of the mirror she gives herself one last inspection. She adjusts her black and gold sequined costume. In the arena the crowd is applauding for a competitor who has just finished her routlne. She knows she is next.

She skates to the entrance of the rink. Coming off the rink is the previous skater who is also her friend. The skaters do not talk to each other. They both know how important it is to concentrate before a routine. She stands next to her coach while the scores begin showing for the last roller skater. The crowd reacts to the fine scores.

Her coach takes her hand. To keep her focused on her routine he talks to her. He says, "You have done this, routine a thousand times and it is perfect." The skater smiles. Her name is announced. She skates to her starting place on the rink. The crowd applauds and then becomes silent. Alone, she stands out in the rink ready to begin.

5

She positions herself, feet together, arms outstretched. Her music begins. As she begins skating, all of her fear disappears. All she can think of now is the music and her routine. She skates her first triple jump without a flaw. Next are several dance steps. As she performs them her personality shows through. They were designed just for her. On the rink the skater realizes how much she enjoys competing. Her enjoyment shows in her smile.

Gliding across the rink, every movement seems effortless. Finally, she finishes with her best move, a flying arabian. Her landing is perfect. She knows she has done her best. She looks to the crowd and sees her parents smiling. They also know she has done her best. The crowd is drawn to their feet. The applause in the arena is deafening. The skater feels on top of the world. She knows she has done her best, and that is all that matters.

The World of Roller Skating

Roller skates have been around for over 200 years. It was not always possible to perform complicated skating tricks. In the very beginning, skaters could not even stop.

The first roller skate was invented by an unknown Dutchman. He attached wooden spools to the bottom of his ice skates. He wanted to be able to skate when the weather was warm.

In 1760, a Belgian man named Joseph Merlin made a pair of roller skates. Merlin was a toolmaker who lived in London. He had been invited to a costume party. To impress all his friends, he entered the party on his roller skates. He tried to play the violin at the same time. Unfortunately, the roller skates were not a big success. The skates Merlin invented could not turn or stop. The only thing that stopped him at the party was a crystal mirror. It shattered into a million pieces after he hit it.

Merlin's skates were not like today's roller skates. The wheels were not lined up in pairs. Merlin's skates had several wheels which ran down the middle from the toe to the heel. They were called in-line skates.

9

The first time roller skates were used successfully was in 1849. A French opera called La Prophe`te contained an ice skating scene. It was not possible to make ice in a theater in those days. A man named Louis Legrange designed skates for the scene. He wanted to make it appear as though the actors were ice skating. Legrange strapped wooden wheels on the bottoms of ice skates. These wheels were all in a line down the middle of the skate like Merlin's skates. Even though the actors could not stop or turn, it allowed them to glide across the stage.

In 1863, James Plimpton invented the roller skate with "rocker action." Plimpton's rocker action allowed the skater to turn. Before this invention, it was necessary to lift one foot off the ground to turn. With rocker action both skates stayed on the ground during a turn. Today, we take this for granted. The people in the 1860s thought it was fantastic.

Plimpton tried to generate interest in roller skating. At first it did not catch on in the United States. Plimpton went to Europe. His ideas caught on in Europe. Soon skating at roller rinks or "**rinking**" was very popular. Americans saw the Europeans rinking and they wanted to do it too.

Roller skating soon became a pastime for the wealthy. They were the only people who could

11

afford to join the rinks. Rinks required people to be a member. This meant paying a fee and not everyone could afford this luxury.

In the late 1800s, there was no outdoor skating. Roads were not paved and skating on an unpaved road was almost impossible.

Plimpton was a good inventor and businessman. He built many rinks and charged skaters membership fees. He also held the **patent** on roller skates. (A patent means that no one else may make or sell your product without your permission.) Plimpton did not sell his skates. Instead, he only leased them to the rinks. This way every time someone skated he made money.

Skating now became fashionable, and many rinks were built. In Chicago, one of the largest rinks, the Casino, had 16,000 square feet and a white maple floor. At this rink there were often 800 to 1,000 people a day skating. They always wore formal clothes, because skating was a social occasion.

Joining a rink was a good way for people to meet. Many women took up roller skating. It was a very respectable way to meet men. Still, there were certain rules women had to follow. Women could not put their skates on in the same place as men.

By the 1880s, Plimpton's patent had run out. More companies then sold skates. They started mass producing skates. This meant the prices dropped. More people could afford to buy them.

In the beginning of the 1900s, people had more spending money. Roller skating was still a favorite pastime and more people joined rinks. If skating was all the rage before, now it had taken the country by storm. In the past, roller skating had been for adults. Now everyone was skating.

New designs also helped make roller skating more popular. Ball bearings were added to the wheels. This made the ride much smoother. Roller skating became so popular that songs and movies were made about it. In 1916, Charlie Chaplin even starred in a movie called *The Rink*. Movie stars kept on skating in their films. Fred Astaire and Ginger Rogers skated in one of their movies, *Shall We Dance* .

It was not until the 1920s that roller skaters hit the pavement. Streets were paved. People began skating outdoors, especially children.

In England, some people wanted to prevent children from roller skating in the streets. They felt it was too dangerous. Winston Churchill, who later became Prime Minister of England, said he

would not take away the recreation of poorer children. They would have nowhere else to go. Churchill became the patron saint of English roller skating.

Skating outdoors started new fads. Endurance skating became very popular. In 1927, Arthur Allegreti skated 390 miles, from Buffalo, New York to New York City. He did this in 58 hours without any sleep. All he ate along the way were hot dogs. A year later, John Balaz skated 1,100 miles in 231 hours. He skated for more than 9 days straight.

During the Great Depression skating was a cheap way to have fun. In 1931 over 2 million skates were sold in the U.S.

In the 1940s, **roller dancing** became popular. Men and women danced together in teams on roller skates.

During World War II, the government encouraged roller skating. It "maintained physical conditioning that is necessary during wartime." There were even suggestions of using roller skates to move troops to the front lines. The idea failed, because skating in the grass or dirt was impossible.

In the 1950s and 1960s roller skating hit a slump. People did not skate as much any more. Instead, skating became a sport for watchers. **Roller derbies** sprang up. The first roller derbies were strictly for endurance. Skaters would line up at the starting line like they do in a running race. Whoever finished first won. During the races, people bumped into each other. From this bumping came roller derbies.

In the 1950s, roller derbies hit their all-time high. They were featured on television. Roller derby programs shared the spot light with popular TV personalities like Milton Berle. Speed and noise made the derby an exciting spectator sport.

Roller skating has come full circle. In-lines have been "re-invented." The original roller skate is making a comeback.

Competitive Skating

Competitive skating has three different categories: artistic skating, speed skating, and roller hockey. These three different types of skating are recognized by the United States Amateur Confederation of Roller Skating **(USAC/RS)**. The USAC/RS is the governing body for roller skating in America. They oversee major competitions. Over 23,000 members and 1,150 roller skating clubs belong to the USAC/RS.

Each of the three different areas of roller skating is divided into two levels of competition: the standard level and the Junior Olympics (JO). JOs help beginning skaters perfect their technical ability and get used to competing. The Junior Olympics now has its own championship every year. It is usually held in the beginning of September. In the Junior Olympics, skaters are grouped by age and ability.

Competitive skating dates back to the early 1800s. Roller rink owners employed professional skaters to skate at their rinks. (A professional athlete gets paid to compete. Amateur athletes do not get paid for competing.) **Professional** skating couples and individuals performed difficult maneuvers on skates. The owners thought this would make people want to learn to skate better. They hoped skaters would buy more lessons.

Between 1900 and 1950, skating acts often toured the country. These acts were very popular in the 1940s. A show was an inexpensive way for people to enjoy themselves during WW II.

A group called the "Skating Vanities" rolled through the country in 1942. Actors in the group wore fancy costumes with sequins and feathers. They performed musicals. At first the country could not imagine a roller skating show. Soon the show was getting rave reviews.

The Skating Vanities toured the U.S. and Europe. In England, one of the skaters, Gloria Nord, was asked to put on a command performance for the Queen.

Show skating opened the door to competitive skating. The three types of competitive skating are very different. They all have one thing in common: they demand athletic ability.

Artistic Skating

Artistic skaters can compete in one or all four of the following events: school figures, singles free skating, pairs, and dance.

School figures (also called roller schools) demand precision. Each skater traces figure patterns (such as a figure "8") painted on the floor. The skater must skate over a line 3/4 of an inch wide. This takes balance, control, and concentration. The skater is judged on compulsory moves. There is no creativity here. The skater also must use take-offs and turns during school figures. It takes keen concentration to stay on track.

Figures were derived from ballet. There are certain moves a dancer must know how to perform. After learning these, the moves are combined along with music to produce a ballet. In 1863, school figures were invented for ice skaters. Later roller skaters also performed these required moves. A skater must know how to do the compulsory moves first. Later the compulsory moves are used in other areas of roller skating.

Singles free skating, or free skating, is set to music. The Skaters interpret the music through dance. Following a specific routine is not a requirement. Singles free skating involves jumps and spins. It is impossible to jump and spin if you do not know the basics. Skaters work on their basics before trying jumps and spins.

Both men and women compete in singles free skating. There is a men's division and a women's division. Each year the number of skaters who compete in free skating increases. The quality and level of competition also increases. At the 53rd United States Roller Skating Competition in 1989, competition for both the men and women was high.

Scott Cohen, a two-time world champion and three-time U.S. champion, was in a slump. He came back, however, to take first place in the men's division. Judges rated Cohen on technical merit and on artistic impression. Technical merit stresses how well a skater jumps and spins. Artistic impression is how well he or she dances. On a scale of 100, Cohen received eight scores of 99 and two scores of 98. The latter was for technical merit. He won the championship. The win makes Cohen a four time U.S. champion.

Pairs skating involves a man and a woman skating together. Pairs skating includes all the spins and jumps of singles skating. It also adds lifts, when one skater picks up his partner. Imagine lifting another person while roller skating at the same time. If you think that is tough, imagine being lifted. And then being put down, and trying to stay on your feet. Pairs skaters do all that and make it look easy. Pairs skating is much like pairs ice skating, except on wheels.

Pairs skaters mirror each other. Part of their routine involves skating next to each other without touching. They each perform the same tricks, side by side. If one skater is spinning, the other skater must be spinning at the same time. It should look like one of them is a mirror image of the other skater. This is made more difficult because team members are not usually the same size.

Many pairs skaters meet when they are young. Often they are paired by their parents or an instructor. The skaters must be able to work with each other and enjoy competing. But most important, is that each skater likes his or her partner.

Skating with a partner involves more sacrifices than skating single. There is always the other person to consider. Once a pair is matched, they usually agree to skate together for at least one year.

The Dance competition is also performed by a man and a woman. Each team must do two segments: _compulsory_ dance and _free_ dance.

As with singles skating, the compulsory part is made up of required moves. Compulsory dance requires that each team perform a set of dances. The teams are then judged.

In free dance, each team may interpret a dance as they wish. They may choose their own music. Each team tries to bring out their own style. Skaters show their personality when they are able to choose their own music and style.

Speed Skating

The gun goes off. Racers sprint until they round the first corner. The noise of the crowd is deafening. Then the skaters settle into stride. The only time racers must stay in their lanes is at the start. During the race, each skater gives it their all until they hit the finish line. After they cross the line they try to regain their breath and get ready for the next race.

Speed skating is pure racing. Racers skate in a pack. Most of the time they are not very graceful. Looks and style do not count on the race course. All that matters is who crossed the finish line first. Skaters line up at the starting line, and each skater has his or her own lane. After they round the first corner, skaters are allowed to skate in any lane. It is a pack race where the quickest and strongest finish first.

Most roller speed skating competitions are held on an indoor track. Each lap is 100 meters. Speed skaters compete in divisions grouped by age. Skaters also compete in individual and relay races. Individual races are scored by how fast each skater skates in several races. They earn 30 points for a win, 20 points for second place, and 10 points for third place. The skater who has the most points wins.

Children five years old and younger skate in the tiny tot division. They skate three races each. The races are 100, 200, and 300 meters. The Juvenile race is for eight and nine-year-olds. They also skate three races up to 500 meters long. Races with the longest distances are in the men's senior division. They skate in four races, and the point total decides the winner. The distances in these races are 1,000, 1,500, 3,000, and 5,000 meters (50 laps).

In a *relay* race, a team skates. The team who has the fastest time wins. Each skater skates a certain number of laps. When the skater gets to the gate area (an area where one team member stops and another begins), they push the next skater. This push is called a tag. Each team member must tag the next person or they are disqualified.

Many speed skaters start training at a very young age. At the nationals in 1989, the youngest skater was six. Speed skating is tough. Skaters put in two hours of training every day. On the national level, skaters put in even more time for training. In addition, they train with weights. Speed skating takes a lot of dedication and a will to win.

Roller Hockey

There are three types of roller hockey: ball hockey, puck hockey and street hockey. Ball hockey and puck hockey are recognized by the USAC/RS. Roller hockey has become the first roller skating event to reach Olympic status. Ball hockey will be a demonstration sport at the 1992 Summer Olympic Games. In demonstration sports, the final score does not count toward a medal. But it is the first step to becoming a medal winning Olympic sport.

Ball hockey is a lot like ice hockey. Participants follow similar rules. Ball hockey is played indoors. Players use a curved stick and a small ball. The ball is made of cork and covered with rubber. Two teams of five members each play. No checking or body contact is allowed. (Checking is when one player hits a player of the opposite team with his body.) The ball is faster in roller ball hockey than in ice hockey. Players play a passing game. The ball can reach speeds of 80 miles per hour. They pass more since they are not permitted to check.

Players wear helmets and shin guards for protection.

Puck hockey is less common in the United States than ball hockey. Hockey players skate

on indoor rinks. Puck hockey is played with standard ice hockey sticks. A collapsible puck made of soft plastic is used. Checking is permitted. In fact it is an important part of the game. Puck hockey is played in the same manner as in the National Hockey League. It is much rougher than ball hockey.

Street hockey is not governed by the USAC/RS. Street hockey is played on many city streets. It is almost like puck hockey, and leagues are formed by people interested in playing. Churches or local merchants often sponsor teams. Street hockey is played on playgrounds with boards forming the boundaries. The Boards are needed to keep the puck from rolling away.

Street hockey is a very aggressive sport. Leagues follow the same rules as the NHL whenever possible. Boys and girls of all ages play. Just as in any other area of roller skating, good skating skills are a must.

Getting Started

Skating is good exercise for everyone. It does not matter if you are a pro athlete or a weekend athlete. Skating has always been a fine way of getting in shape. Roller skating is an aerobic activity. Aerobics help increase the amount of oxygen your body can process. This is good for your lungs and heart.

Skating provides the same physical benefits as swimming or cross-country skiing. It is relatively injury free. Injuries, in general, only occur during a fall. Athletes can train without the worry of muscle pulls. This makes skating ideal for cross training.

What should you look for when renting or buying a pair of skates? It all depends on what you need. Serious skating demands professional skates. If you are just out to have fun, try renting roller skates the first few times. Make sure you like the sport. Skates can be a big investment.

In any skate there are three things to look for, whether you are renting or buying: fit, boot quality, and wheel action.

A skate should fit comfortably. The boot should fit snugly over a thin sock. Boots tend to run one to two sizes smaller than street shoes. Try on

several sizes and widths until you find one that feels right. The fit should be snug enough in the back so your heel does not ride up. It should be roomy enough to allow your toes to wiggle. This helps your circulation. Make sure your boots fit correctly. If not, return them. Skating with a boot that is too small or too big will hurt.

The boot should have support built into the arch. If you are renting skates, ask for the newest pair. They will have the most support. Make sure the laces are not too worn. Otherwise, they may break while you are skating.

Make sure the wheel action is not too loose. If you are not sure, ask someone who knows. It is better for a beginner to have wheels with less action. The less action, the less likely the skate will turn unexpectedly. If you are renting skates, ask the attendant to adjust the action. Having your skates in good working order makes for a better roll.

Now you are ready to roll. You can skate in a rink or outside. Each is a little bit different—so be prepared.

Skating in a rink is a lot of fun. Going with a friend is a good idea. Wear sturdy clothes, like jeans. Most people fall their first time, so wear something that will help cushion the fall.

Out on the rink, stay near the barrier the first few times around. Grab on if you feel yourself falling. Try to relax. You will have better posture if you relax.

When skating outside, most of the same rules apply. If you have never skated, bring a friend who is not on skates. You will have someone steady to grab onto. Wear elbow pads, knee pads, and gloves. All this padding will make the first few falls easier and safer. If you feel yourself falling, do not put your hands out to brace yourself. This can caused sprained wrists. Try to roll with the fall.

Skate rentals for outdoors are around $5.00 for the first hour and $2.50 each additional hour. Most rentals require a drivers license. You may need to bring an adult. Some stores may rent in-line skates. They cost the same as conventional ones. If you have never skated on them try a pair. Beware, next time, it may be a tough decision which skates to choose.

Skating Games

Skating is habit forming. Once you start, it is hard to stop. Outdoor skating does not have to be limited to skating around the block. There are many games you can play. On the following pages are some games you can play with items found around the house.

Limbo - All you need to play is a bar and three people. A broom or mop handle is fine. One person holds an end of the bar while the third player limbos under it. Each time the person makes it under without touching the bar, the bar gets lowered. The player must always go under the bar feet first, with their stomachs facing up .

Slalom - You need six to twelve small items to use as markers. Milk cartons, soda cans, or paper cups will do. Put a little sand or dirt in the bottom to keep them in place. Place the markers at ten-foot intervals along a straight line. To begin, skate and zig zag through the markers. As time goes on, decrease the space between the markers. This will make the course more difficult.

To add variety, go through the course in different positions, or on a downhill slope. If several people are playing, see who can complete the course in the fastest time.

Roller Frisbee - This is like regular frisbee but on roller skates. Feel free to make up rules. The person throwing the frisbee might throw as far as he can. Whoever catches the most frisbees at the farthest point wins.

Shuttle - Two garbage cans are needed (or mark off two circular areas). Divide all the players up into teams. The players all at once race to a single pile of blocks or balls. Each player carries one block back to his team's garbage can and puts the block in there. When all the blocks are gone the team with the most blocks wins.

Skating is a lot of fun. Beginners and experts both find challenges in different types of skating. It has been enjoyed by adults as well as children for the past century. Whether competing or simply out for a roll with friends, roller skating has something for everyone. The only rule is to have fun.

Glossary

Artistic Skating: A competition that can include school figures, singles free skating, pairs or dance skating.

Ball Hockey: An indoor hockey game played with roller skates instead of ice skates. Players use a curved stick and a small ball. Each team has five players.

Dance Competition: Team skating which includes required dances and free dance, where the skaters can make up their own dances.

In-line Skates: Skates that have their wheels lined up between the toe and heel instead of two wheels on each side.

Junior Olympics: Called JO, a division of skating competition that helps beginners perfect their technical skating ability.

Pair Skating: A man and woman skating team. It includes spins, jumps and one skater lifting another.

Patent: Protects an inventors idea. No one can sell a product that has been patented without the permission of the inventor.

Professional: An athlete that gets paid to compete.

Puck Hockey: Played with regular hockey sticks. A rougher game than ball hockey.

Rinking: Skating at a skating rink.

Roller Dancing: Men and women dancing together in teams on roller skates.

Roller Derbies: A race on roller skates. The skaters try to bump the other skaters out of their way.

School Figure: Also called roller schools. The skater traces over lines on the floor —like a figure 8.

Singles Free: Skating to music. The skaters interpret the music by dancing with their skates on.

Speed Skating: A skating race. The winner is the first to cross the finish line.

Street Hockey: Like puck hockey, but played on the street.

USAC/RS: The United States Amateur Confederation of Roller Skating. They oversee major competitions.